THE

FINE

OLD TREE

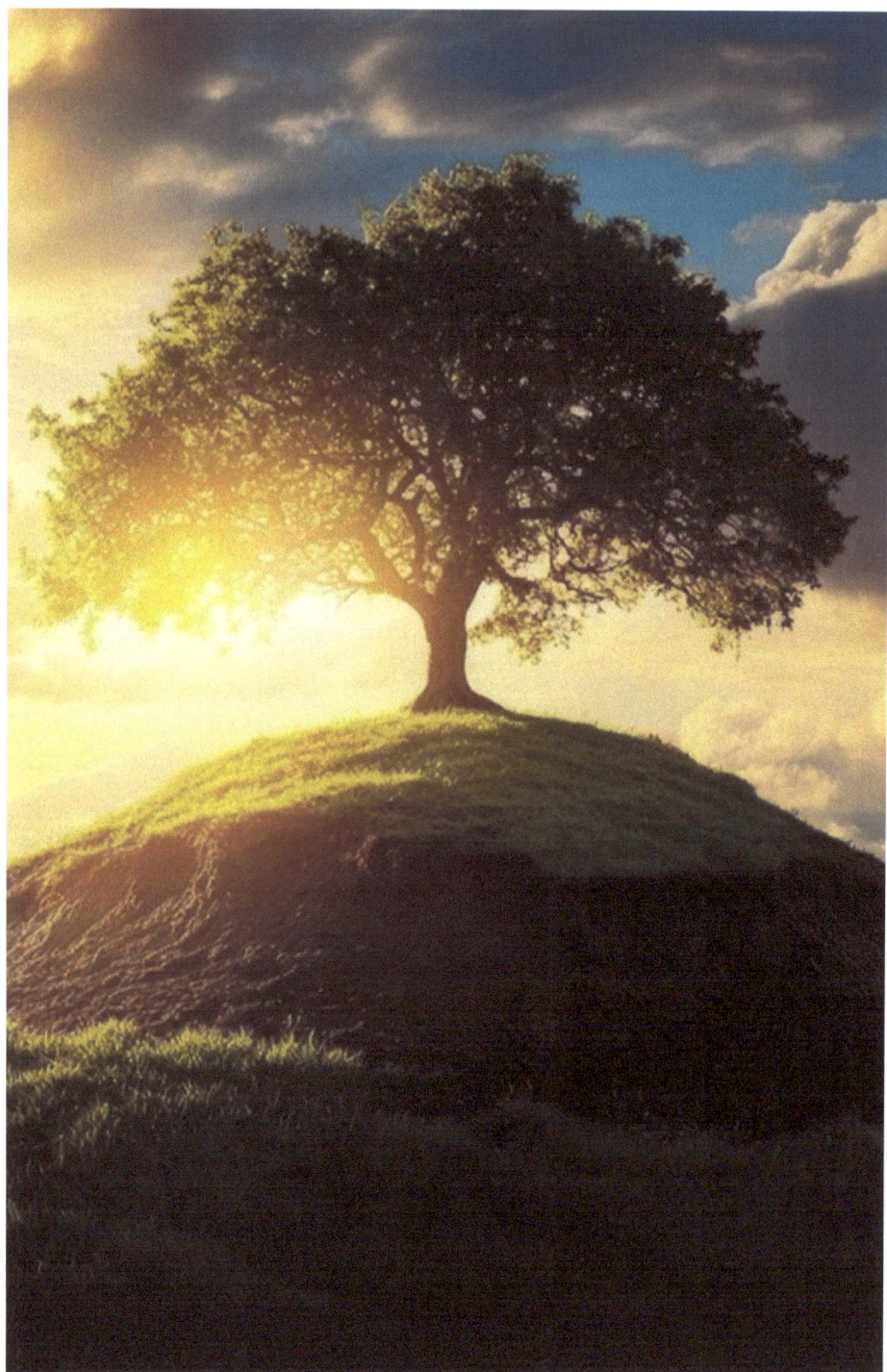

OUR GUIDING LIGHT

THE HOLY SPIRIT

THE FINE OLD TREE

ACKNOWLEDGEMENTS

First and foremost, I thank God for His guidance in writing this book. It is only by His grace that this work exists.

To my wife, Penny—your love, patience, and unwavering support have been my greatest blessing.

To my children, Robert, Joel, and Sara—your insights and encouragement have strengthened this book in countless ways.

To my brother, Dr. Bruce Hartman—your wisdom, support, and belief in me have meant more than words can express.

To Pastor Sam Caldwell—thank you for your prayers and guidance.

To the people of Deering Center Community Church—your encouragement and prayers have lifted me up throughout this journey.

To my parents Bob and Dot – thank you for exposing me to the Lord and his church

With deep gratitude,
James Hartman

ABOUT THE AUTHOR

James Hartman is a retired businessman, devoted family man, and lifelong mentor from Portland, Maine. Married for 50 years, he has three children and seven grandchildren. A dedicated Elder at Deering Center Community Church, he also serves on the Maine Bible Society Board and has led Habitat for Humanity Maine. With 37 years of coaching experience, including 20 years as a high school football head coach, he has mentored thousands of young athletes. Now, as the author of *The Fine Old Tree*, he shares spirit-led poetry on faith, redemption, and the power of the Cross.

This book is written for those who believe in our Lord Jesus Christ.

The Holy Spirit has come to me and asked me to write this book. The Holy Spirit told me that he is grieving for his Church. The Holy Spirit is concerned that his Church (believers in Jesus as Lord) do not understand the absolute importance of the Cross of Jesus Christ!

I have written the book as I was led by the Holy Spirit.

Jim Hartman

The picture is of a mustard tree.

THE FINE OLD TREE

Look at the Fine Old Tree so beautiful with such a
large, expansive, canopy overshadowing all, with all
the flying creatures finding comfort and rest in her
branches, all creatures come and find comfort and rest
in her shade.

The Fine Old Tree cries out to all men Come!
Come those who are hurting.
Come those who are deaf and blind
Come those who are poor
Come those who are oppressed
Come put away your hard work and find rest in my
shade
Come and let a cool refreshing breeze flow over you

Press into the Fine Old Tree
And be healed
Find comfort and peace in me
And I will lead you and take care of you
Open your eyes and ears to the river flowing from me
Refresh yourselves in the cool refreshing waters
flowing from the Fine Old Tree
eat of the leaves from the fruit trees lining the banks
of the refreshing river

What a Fine Old Tree we have

THE FINE OLD TREE

Alas, so much darkness surrounds us.
So much poverty
So much heartbreak
So much pain
So much desire for another way!

So I went in search of another way
Along the way
I was met by an old man with a white beard
I asked him where to find the better way
He smiled and just pointed to the much better way

I looked and saw a mountain with a small glimmer of
light atop it
I stared at the light with desire and wonderment

While running to the light
A gentle breeze whispered to me
Come unto me!
As I quickly moved up the mountain the light got
brighter
The breeze shouted louder "Come unto me"

As I near the top I could see the light
It was coming from a Fine Old Tree
What a beautiful Fine Old Tree!
So full of life!

I was almost upon the Fine Old Tree

THE FINE OLD TREE

When I could see something red running down its
trunk
The gentle breeze whispered come unto The Fine Old
Tree and touch me
So, like a child, I put my fingers into the Red Flow
And upon touching the Red Flow
my whole body was pulled into the Red Flow.

I felt so cleansed
I was filled with so much peace
So much joy
So much love
So much desire for the Fine Old Tree
And the Red Flow
Finally, everywhere there was comfort and peace!

OH, what a Fine Old Tree!

THE FINE OLD TREE

I gazed upon the tree.
In awe and
In wonderment

There was such a spirit of peace and tranquility in the
air
It must be a tree of such importance
Yes, indeed a very special tree!
A Very Fine Old Tree

I looked upon the birds flocking to the Fine Old Tree
and I noticed the child playing with a cobra
and the Lamb lying with the Lion in its shade!

Why is it so special?
What secrets does it hold?

Out of a sweet gentle breeze, I heard
Look at the nails in the tree which held up the Truth
Look at the Red Flow and water flowing from the
Fine Old Tree
Look at the crown on its branches
Look at the sign that says King of Kings

The gentle breeze declared this Fine Old Tree is
the Marker for all of mankind to decide about the
Truth!
It is Strength for those that love the Truth!
It is Grace for those that know the Truth!

THE FINE OLD TREE

It is Healing for those that believe the Truth!
It is Power for those that walk with the Truth!"

What is this Truth I asked?
The gentle breeze answered.
He is waiting for you!
Go and seek Him
Sit on His knee and
He will show you all things!!"

I am going but first, what is that Red Flow
The Red Flow is His!
"It was what the Truth used to purchase men for the
great "I AM"

Oh my! What a Fine Old Tree

THE FINE OLD TREE

Can anyone help us, please?
We are seeking the Rabbi can you tell us where He is?
We had heard His voice on the Mount
and Oh My, how beautiful His voice is,
and with so much authority!
Oh my, we must find Him!

Oh, I am so sorry a gentle breeze whispered to me,
the soldiers just took Him
Where did they take him? We must find Him
The gentle breeze whispered
"The soldiers took him out the east gate and up to
Golgotha"

Running towards Golgotha we found all was quiet
There were just 2 Roman soldiers guarding an open
tomb
Oh my! we are too late

Oh, so heartbroken
And we then looked up and saw a magnificent Fine
Old Tree
While we gaze upon the Fine Old Tree
We noticed the Red Flow coming from the tree and
a prophet from old dressed in a fine white robe
standing there

Sir, can you help us find Him?
We are so in distress that we cannot find Him

THE FINE OLD TREE

Then the prophet said he was nailed to the tree and
the Red Flow is His
We were crushed!

Then he said do not cry; for He was nailed to the tree
for you!
And He has risen for you!

OH, how will we ever find Him?
The prophet led us to the Red Flow and told us to
wash our dirty clothes in the Red Flow
We were puzzled but we did it
Oh my! Our clothes turned bright white and
Oh! What a feeling of peace and calm

Just then there was the Rabbi standing to our right
We held the Rabbi tightly
Oh! what peace and joy
All of sudden the Rabbi took us to the throne of God.

Oh, what a magnificent Fine Old Tree it is

THE FINE OLD TREE

*"Where we will serve him day and night
in his temple and he who sits on the throne will spread his
tent over them.*

*Never again will they hunger; never again will they thirst.
The sun will not beat upon them, nor any scorching heat.*

*For the Lamb at the center of the throne will be their
shepherd; he will lead them to springs of living water.
And God will wipe away every tear from their eyes."*

Revelation 7:15

THE FINE OLD TREE

"Could Be an Autobiography"

As I was nearing the finish line
I came to a fork in the road
I looked up and saw the Fine Old Tree that was
dividing the road.
Now in sight of the fork, I saw that each road had a
finish line.
How sad I thought when I saw that the right fork was
narrow and had a gate.
Oh, but how grand was the fork to the left
Lined with riches, cheering crowds, and lots of
adulation
Just have to work harder to cross the finish line first.

Oh, I did it. Look at me, I am the best!
Lots of prizes and slaps on the back
But woe is me, how empty, how soon did the
adulations end
The crowd went back to their lives and left me
standing there with all my prizes, and then the prizes
soon turned to dust.
What happened, where is that feeling of glory
Oh! The emptiness!

I have to rid myself of this emptiness.
I know what, I will run the race again and they will
all see how great I am.
I will work hard and harder.
The race started and soon enough I was ahead.

THE FINE OLD TREE

Oh, how special am I!

As I came up to the fork I was way ahead of the
others
The Fine Old Tree drew my eyes to it and it beckoned
to me
I stopped and gazed at the tree and I noticed the Red
Flow coming from it.
The tree pointed to the narrow fork in the road
And then I saw a man in a White Robe.
I almost fell to the ground looking at him but I saved
myself.
I saw that the man in the White Robe was leading an
old woman and a young child
thru the gate.
Wow, I have never seen such beauty.
Oh, such peace in the Gentle Breeze that was calling
my name.

But then I heard the cry of crowd and all of its
adulations screaming for me.
I remembered all the prizes, the claps on my back,
and my pride rose up.
I quickly took the left fork and ran to all that awaited
me with my sure victory.
But alas! The same darkness and lies were my reward.
So Empty!

What am I doing wrong?

THE FINE OLD TREE

Maybe I did not work hard enough. I will work
harder.
This time I will win by a much bigger distance.
So, I started running harder and I was invincible or so
I thought.
Way ahead! But oh, the hard work and chaos, is it
worth it?
Then the Gentle Breeze spoke firmly "Find your Rest
at the foot of the Fine Old Tree"

As I approached the fork in the road from a distance I
became to ponder the Fine Old Tree.
I thought about the beauty and the peace that was in
the Gentle Breeze.
I hoped I would see the man in the White Robe again.
My thoughts went back again to how nobody could
catch me.

What is this?
Oh My! What feeling of warmth and peace has come
over me!
All of a sudden, he was beside me
running stride for stride with me and I felt him
piercing my soul.
Oh! What a feeling of rest, I took a deep breath and
sighed.
What is your name I inquired?
I am the Alpha and the Omega.

THE FINE OLD TREE

For some reason, I could barely hear the adulation of
the crowd now.

I asked him if he would take me to the gate.
His voice so gentle and sweet said
first, let me show you my nails in the Fine Old Tree.

As we approached the Fine Old Tree.
I saw the nails and I peered at the Red Flow coming
from the Fine Old Tree
and asked him what is that Red Flow.
He answered that is my Red Flow. I left it for you.
Why I wondered
The Red Flow is for your cleansing, he whispered into
my heart.
The Red Flow will take away the darkness, the
emptiness and will fill you with my spirit.
Oh, let me bathe in it.
Oh, I feel so clean and rested!

He put his arm around me and led me down the
narrow fork in the road.
As we approached the gate he was no longer by my
side.
But I could still feel him, how could this be?
When we stood in front of the gate
I could feel my tongue sticking to the roof of my
mouth

THE FINE OLD TREE

and I felt his voice coming from out my soul,
thundering for the gate to open.

As I crossed the finish line of the gate, I saw the
immense beauty of his house!

Oh! How wonderful that Fine Old Tree and the Red
Flow of His is!

What a Fine Old Tree

THE FINE OLD TREE

HE turned to Abraham and pointed to a beautiful
young girl named Mary.

Mary was entering a building with a tall white spire
pointing to heaven.
The building was beautiful, modern, and even had a
tree hanging in the corner.
She sat in the same spot she had for 18 years every
Sunday morning.
Mary listened and watched every Sunday knowing
that for some reason she just had to be there.

Saddened HE remarked to Abraham,
"The man in the pulpit did not tell Mary to find me
and my tree".
So, I could make her my daughter!

The ravages of the world started to creep in on Mary.
Telling her she was not worthy. A spirit of depression
and darkness slowly crept into Mary.

Mary went off to college and deeper into the world,
but HE always kept HIS eyes on her, hoping to be
invited into her life.
Mary was working harder and harder trying to find
some purpose
HE did his best to help Mary but HIS hands were tied
Mary was so busy trying to feel worthy and wanted,
she had no time to hear about HIM.

THE FINE OLD TREE

As the years went by Mary was married and had a
beautiful family
There were 2 houses, one even on the shore.
The world let her think that she was great and
accomplishing much.
But Mary still felt a gigantic hole in her heart.

Eventually, HE was able to remind Mary about the
building with a white spire.
Mary went to the building and went in and looked
around.
Oh so sad, it was the same building she knew from 40
years ago
Same old empty words and lifeless people
Mary knew she had to flee!

As the years went by Mary tried many different
buildings
but it was the same everywhere she went,
The men in the pulpit of the buildings just kept
preaching Peace Peace and emptiness.
Some buildings did not even have a Tree hanging in
the corner.
They were all so empty and devoid of light.

HE was so dismayed
For no one had told Mary about HIM or HIS tree.
HE longed to help her but could not.

THE FINE OLD TREE

For Mary had no knowledge of HIM or faith in HIM.

The years kept creeping by.
Mary was now 75 years old and, in more loneliness,
darkness, pain, and fear than ever!
Something just had to be done quickly!
So, HE put it on Mary's heart to go for a walk in HIS
forest.
Knowing HE could meet her there.
As Mary wandered thru the forest her soul started to
be quiet
and long for something that Mary could not
understand.
Even though she did not know what it was Mary
knew she had to find it.
As Mary dashed off to find what was causing her soul
to burn.
The scales started to slip off her eyes and HIS light
became brighter.

Over there look at that light
Oh, how peaceful and wonderful everything is over
there!
Then her soul quickened and pointed her to the Fine
Old Tree.

Instantly Mary knew this tree was special and might
be her longed-for answer.

THE FINE OLD TREE

Mary went to the Fine Old Tree and sat down and
thought
Oh, what peace there is here!
Then Mary saw a Red Flow Flowing from the Fine
Old tree
curiously she reached out and just touched the Red
Flow
In an instance, the scales fell completely from Mary's
eyes
her heart raced
her soul jumped for Joy
her heart was now available to Him,
HE was now able to speak into Mary's heart.

Upon seeing HIM
She asked HIM what is the Red Flow coming from the
Fine Old Tree,
HE told her it was a gift from me to you.
Go bathe yourself in the Red Flow and be set free.

As Mary felt the Red Flow that was flowing over her
her chains of bondage fell from her.
Gone forever is the fear and pain.
HE told me now all my past is gone and forgotten.
I AM now your future
Oh! So wonderful

Oh wow! How bitterly sad to have discovered HIM at
75 years of age.

THE FINE OLD TREE

Why did I have to waste all those years of not
knowing HIM
Why oh why did no one tell me about HIM and The
Fine Old Tree?

As I turned to go, I turned back to look at The Fine
Old Tree one more time.
It will be all right now for I can and will come to HIs
Fine Old Tree every day!

Oh My!

What a Great God!

What a Fine Old Tree I have!

THE FINE OLD TREE

Walking to the fish market as I do most days,
stopping at a familiar place on the mount to rest I
thought
It is so peaceful here!
Songbirds flying in and about the Fine Old Tree
What beauty!
But alas I must be off to town
Oh! How I dread leaving this spot for what awaits me
in the town.

A few days later going to the market,
As I approached the mount, I was daydreaming about
the mount and its peace.
But, Oh my! What is happening?
so many soldiers
so many people shouting
and a sign on the Fine Old Tree saying "King of
Kings"
Oh My! there is a man all bloodied nailed to the tree.
I must go quickly; I cannot get caught up in what is
happening here.

Later on, that fateful day as I was leaving the market
there was so much darkness for the sun was gone
and all of a sudden shouts were coming from the
temple
Something about a curtain
My feet went out from under me as the road opened
up and split apart

THE FINE OLD TREE

Must get home
Must avoid the mount and turmoil

Months went by after that dreadful day,
The world became harsher and more cruel
All peace had gone
I had heard something about the man on the tree and
the peace that HE was offering.
But I just could not understand what was being said.

Oh, how I need peace and calm
I know, I will walk by the Fine Old Tree today
Let's hope the chaos from that day is gone
As I came upon the Fine Old Tree
everything looked new and more peaceful.

The Fine Old Tree now had the door in its trunk
which folks were using.
Behind the Fine Old Tree was a road
A very straight road, so clean, no hills and a small
gate at the end.
As I stared in amazement, I noticed that the folks
going to the door
were old, crippled, or needed help.
Then I saw a man opening the door for someone to go
thru the door
but then he would not open the door for someone else

THE FINE OLD TREE

Just had to get to the door and to ask him what was
happening.
As I got closer, I could see that those who went thru
the door were skipping and running now!
Oh! How joyful they looked.
When I asked the man at the door where those who
were walking on the straight and narrow road were
going?
He smiled kindly and said to the Father's House, to
live in peace forever.
But what about these others who cannot go through
the door I asked.
He sadly said that they had not cleansed themselves.
Oh My, I thought to myself I must go and wash
myself.
But knowing my thoughts the man told me that is not
how it works,
only the Man that was nailed to the Fine Old Tree can
wash you.
Oh My, I was at a loss as to what to do.
But thankfully a gentle breeze came and whispered
into my soul
"Go and seek Him and He will come unto you"

Puzzled and saddened I walked away back toward
the world
Oh, I do not want to go back into the world!

Hurrying here and there to find him

THE FINE OLD TREE

until I was exhausted and broken and I fell to my
knees and wept!
All of a sudden, I heard my name being called
and my soul awoke inside me.
I looked up into the most beautiful sight my eyes
could ever see, so pure, so bright!
Oh, I felt so unworthy and dirty that I collapsed
before Him.

He picked me up and peered so deeply into my soul
Oh, I am burning all over.
I did not have to ask if He was the one I sought.
I asked Him if he would cleanse me.
He said yes and He carried me to the Fine Old Tree
Oh, Thank You!

His nails were still in the tree and there was a strange
Red Flow
What is that Red Flow I asked.
He replied it was his Red Flow. It is for you to cleanse
yourself with.

After he had washed me
I started for the door, for I desperately wanted to go
down the narrow road.
But He stopped me and said no you cannot go yet.
I need you to go and proclaim what I have done for
you to others.

THE FINE OLD TREE

When you are done, I will carry you thru the door in
the Fine Old Tree
and I will bring you to my father myself.
Then we will eat at the banquet table together.

Now go and whatever you ask for in my name will be
yours!

Oh! How awesome is the King of Kings

And

How Great the Fine Old Tree is!

THE FINE OLD TREE

As His Word moved out from His throne
HE spoke and a new universe was born.

On the third planet from the sun,
And on the third day that The Word had created
The Word seeded His planet.

The first seed The Word planted was a mustard seed,
(as the mustard tree will grow into the biggest tree in
the garden).
The Word planted this seed on Mt. Moriah
Which is the center of the universe!

The Word took great care of His new creation.
The Word took special care of the mustard seed,
watering the seed Himself
while visiting it as much as He could.

On a visit to His mustard seed one day
The Word noticed that the seed had grown into a Fine
Old Tree.
With birds of the air perched in its shade.

One fine day centuries later when a righteous man
named Abram returned from a battle with 4 kings
The Word went out to meet Abram and promised that
He would be Abram's shield forever.
The Word told Abram that Abram's seed would
inherit forever the land where the mustard tree grew.

THE FINE OLD TREE

Some years later The Word as a test asked Abram to
sacrifice his son on Mount Moriah
So, Abram and his promised son Isaac walked slowly
up Mt. Moriah.
For on Mt. Moriah Abram was prepared to obey The
Word
and to sacrifice his only son to Him.

As Abram was ready and started to use the knife to
sacrifice Isaac,
The Word saw that Abram had made the right choice
in faith
and The Word was pleased with Abram.
Then The Word stopped Abram from using the knife
on Isaac
And then The Word himself provided the sacrifice!

As the centuries continued on,
David (Abraham's seed) during a plague bought the
top of Mount Moriah
so that by a sacrifice the plague would be stopped.
A few years later David's seed built a home for The
Word on the top of Mount Moriah.

The Word kept on caring for the seed, watering and
feeding it Himself.
The seed grew into a Fine Old Tree
Then the day came that had been long planned for,

THE FINE OLD TREE

and the Fine Old Tree was needed.
For this day was to be a tough day for The Great I AM
and The Word.

For out of the Great I AM's pure love for His creation,
HE was going to give the world a chance to be with
HIM forever,
So, on this day HE sacrificed HIS own Son on the Fine
Old Tree.
As The Word's Red Flow flowed down the Fine Old
Tree
The Word would now be able to forgive and forget all
the mistakes ever made
by all those who believed in Him.

What a Fine Old Tree we have!

THE FINE OLD TREE

Who has believed our report?
And to whom has the arm of the Lord been revealed?
2 For He shall grow up before Him as a tender plant,
And as a root out of dry ground.
He has no form or comeliness;
And when we see Him,
There is no beauty that we should desire Him.
3 He is despised and rejected by men,
A Man of sorrows and acquainted with grief.
And we hid, as it were, our faces from Him;
He was despised, and we did not esteem Him.
4 Surely He has borne our griefs
And carried our sorrows;
Yet we esteemed Him stricken,
Smitten by God, and afflicted.
5 But He was wounded for our transgressions,
He was bruised for our iniquities;
The chastisement for our peace was upon Him,
And by His stripes, we are healed.
6 All we like sheep have gone astray;
We have turned, everyone, to his own way;
And the Lord has laid on Him the iniquity of us all.

Isaiah 53: 1-6

THE FINE OLD TREE

Oh My! That poor man!
Whom they nailed to the Fine Old Tree
How sad they have torn his beard out
So disfigured and beaten beyond recognition
Was it necessary for those thorns in his head?
So much blood coming from the thorns, nails and the
spear in his side.

When I pondered so mournfully about who it was on
the Fine Old Tree
and why did this happen to Him?
I heard a voice in a cloud telling me
"This is My Son whom I Love.
Listen to him!"

I strained to hear the Son but with so much confusion
and yelling it was hard to hear him.
Oh! the fancy robed men were mocking him so badly.
Something about saving himself and building a
temple.
So mean and arrogant.
Oh! Leave him alone I cried out.

But then, a voice was coming from the Fine Old Tree
"Father forgive them for they do not know what they
are doing"
Wow, what Grace and Love!

Still, another voice spoke out from another Tree.

THE FINE OLD TREE

Something about repenting
The Son answered the man on the other tree
with incredible forgiveness;
"I tell you the truth, today you will be with Me in
paradise"

The Son looked down and saw a woman and a man
under the Fine Old Tree.
By her reactions, she must have been his mother.
Then the Son said to her
"Dear women, here is your son and
to the man, here is your mother"
All that pain and He is still thinking of others.

Who is this man on the Fine Old Tree?

Again, I heard the voice saying to me
"God is now crushing him with all of sins of the
world
from the past to the present and the future."
And then it was now the sixth hour and
darkness came over the whole land until the ninth
hour.
The Son shouted, "My God, My God, why have you
forsaken me?"

And when knowing all was completed
and so that was written about Him would be fulfilled.
The Son said "I am thirsty"

THE FINE OLD TREE

So, a soldier with a sponge on a stalk of hyssop
offered him a drink.

When the Son had received the drink he lowered his
head and said
"IT IS FINISHED"

Then there were shouts coming from the temple
something about the curtain being torn in half.
I fell as a major earthquake struck the Old City.
Seeing all that was happening the gentile in charge
praised God and said surely this was The Son of God!

I hurried to escape. I felt so alone and terrified.
For months I was so confused and fearful.
But then The Son graciously came to me at night
and stood at the end of my bed and told me,
the scene at the Fine Old Tree was for your cleansing.
And when you have washed in the Red Flow coming
from the Fine old Tree
you will not need to fear anymore for I will be with
you forever.

The Son as he left then said "I am the way, the truth
and the life."

What a Fine Old tree we have!

THE FINE OLD TREE

Still in confusion from what had happened here in the
Old City
and then looking over at Golgotha I noticed an
intriguing older man
sitting above the spot where it happened.

Going over to him, I noticed he could see Golgotha
and the tomb also.
He patted the ground next to him for me to sit down
with him.

The man was so relaxed and quiet that I wondered
how he could be
with what had just happened here.
I finally asked him if he knew what had happened.
Yes, he softly said and he said that he was in on the
planning of it.
Puzzled because clearly, he was not a rabbi or a
Roman soldier
I wondered what he meant.

So, I asked him did you know the man that was
nailed to the Fine Old Tree?
Yes, He was a dear old friend.
In fact, Moses and I just met with Him on the
mountain to plan for His departure.
I also came about 33 years ago to prepare the way for
Him,
to give his people the knowledge of salvation

THE FINE OLD TREE

through the forgiveness of their sins.

Wait a minute, what are you saying? Who are you?
We thought He was the savior of Israel but now that
is not going to happen.

The old man quickly replied, He was and is the savior
of all.
Huh, what do you mean, who are you? Who was he?
So many questions!
The old man replied I am a prophet from old.
and HE was who HE said HE was.
"That HE is in the Father and the Father is in HIM"!

I said, now I am really confused, this is all so hard!
Can you help me to understand more clearly?
Peering deeply into my eyes the old man said, HE IS
the Son of God!
No, it can't be why would someone of that position
allow all of this to happen to him?
To be beaten beyond recognition and to have his
beard pulled out
And then have his blood spilled everywhere as he
was nailed to that Fine Old Tree.

The old man said, because of his incredible and
passionate love for you and all of the world,
he allowed himself to be the perfect sacrifice for all
man's sins.

THE FINE OLD TREE

Wow, what does this all mean?
Replying he said, so that by nailing Himself to the
Fine Old Tree
You may live in Him forever in His mansion.
If you will only come to Him and believe in Him.

Where do I find him?
Go and call on the name of Jesus and he will find you!

What a Fine Old Tree we have!

THE FINE OLD TREE

He was oppressed and He was afflicted,
Yet He opened not His mouth;
He was led as a lamb to the slaughter,
And as a sheep before its shearers is silent,
So He opened not His mouth.
[8] He was taken from [o]prison and from judgment,
And who will declare His generation?
For He was cut off from the land of the living;
For the transgressions of My people, He was stricken.
[9] And [p]they made His grave with the wicked –
But with the rich at His death,
Because He had done no violence,
Nor was any deceit in His mouth.

Isaiah 53: 7-9

THE FINE OLD TREE

Oh! My soul is so tortured!
What do I do?
Where to turn?
I feel so awful, dirty, and sorrowful!

Venturing onto the hills around Jerusalem
with tears flowing
and not paying any attention to anything but myself
I almost knocked the young man over.

The young man greeted me with a beautiful smile.
His eyes were so clear and full of light.
When he clutched my hand there was so much
warmth,
and I could sense the peace that surrounded him.
His voice was so calming!
I thought to myself why is he so different
how do I find the peace and joy that he has?

All of sudden I could feel his soul peering into my
soul.
The young man looked me in the eyes
and I was burning inside with desire for something
but what is it?
With a knowing smile, he said go and seek the one
who lives in me.
For if you seek Him he will knock on the door, and
He will come in.

THE FINE OLD TREE

Full of tears again I said I am so dirty and full of
darkness,
why would he even come near me?
He asked me are you aware of Paul of Taurus and
what he is doing these days.
Yes, I am aware of Paul and all of his good deeds.

Well take heart, Paul was the greatest persecutor of
the One living in me.
And yet the One living in me healed and forgave
Paul.
Also, do not forget the murderer Moses
The one living in me healed and forgave Moses and
called Moses a man after my own heart
The same for King David.

Oh my! Would he heal me? Where do I find Him?
The young man replied on Calvary
and then he turned and walked up the hill.
I know the Fine Old Tree is on the hill
But I didn't think there was a Calvary on the hill.
But I trusted the young man and followed him up the
hill.
Hoping to find what I needed.

Then the young man to my surprise pointed to The
Fine Old Tree.
When I looked at it I could feel the Fine Old Tree
pulling me to itself.

THE FINE OLD TREE

As I walked to the Fine Old Tree, I thought what is
this Calvary?
Then I saw a Man in a white robe,
maybe the Man in the white robe could tell me about
Calvary.

Seemly knowing my thoughts, he smiled, and when
he spoke,
I fell to my knees.
Oh, I am so dirty so filthy I can't look up at Him.
He touched and told me to stand up and as I stood
up.
He rose slowly off of the ground and spoke into my
soul,
look at the nails that are now in the Fine Old Tree,
the holes in my hands, and the Red Flow on the Fine
Old Tree.
Calvary is about Me nailing Myself to the Fine Old
Tree
as a sacrifice for all men to cleanse themselves in so
that
I could come and dwell within them.

He said to me remember the forgiveness that was
extended
to your brothers Paul, Moses, and David for their
cleansing.
Come and I will cleanse yourself also in the Red Flow.
Yes Yes!

THE FINE OLD TREE

Oh, how wonderful I feel, I am now full of peace and
joy
And my soul felt so refreshed and my clothes are so
white now!

I jumped up in joy and looked up to thank Him
but he was gone.
I shouted thank you, hoping he would hear me.

Nothing but silence. Then I heard His voice coming
from inside my soul,
saying trust in what has happened today at the Fine
Old Tree,
stay steadfast in Me always and someday I will eat
with you
at the banquet in my Father's mansion.

What a Fine Old Tree I have!

THE FINE OLD TREE

Tired and needing rest, I finally arrived at the top of
the mount.
As I sat down to rest on the mount
my eyes were drawn to the beautiful old Mustard
tree.
So beautiful and spacious, as its branches spread out
far and wide,
with so many birds resting in it.
I thought to myself this must be a very special tree.

A gentle breeze came and whispered to me this tree is
The Fine Old Tree
and it has been the focal point for so many for over
two thousand years.

Closing my eyes as I was reflecting on what the
breeze had told me.
When all of sudden I noticed a bright light,
opening my eyes I saw a very bright ball of light
rising over The Fine Old tree.
When in awe of what I saw before me, a voice came
from the light,
saying this is my tree, and yes, this Fine Old Tree is a
very special tree.
Let Me tell you why.

First and foremost, my tree was where the greatest act
of pure and true LOVE took place.
My Son left My mansion

THE FINE OLD TREE

and nailed Himself to the Fine Old Tree, shedding His
blood on the Fine Old Tree
and emptying all of himself on the tree, so that all
might have everlasting life!
And so that who would ever believe <u>IN</u> Him would
be set free and He would give them Himself.

He even sacrificed himself for his enemies.

Please remember that this Fine Old Tree and His
blood on it belongs to each and every one of you!

When My Son died on the tree, He was able to fulfill
all of His words;

When he died on the tree, He enabled the Great
Counselor to come to those who believed.
The Great Counselor will unleash the Son's power
into all who believe.
and please remember the Counselor is still now
available to you
and to those who believe <u>IN</u> My Son.

This Fine Old Tree is the MARKER for all of
humanity!
For all of humanity will have to choose to believe IN
Him or not to believe!
For My word says "all knees will bow to Him"

THE FINE OLD TREE

Careful! whichever way you choose will determine
where you will spend eternity!

Oh my! When My Son chose to die on the Fine Old
Tree, He obtained Victory for all!
He conquered DEATH for all who believe IN Him.

It was so special to watch Him deliver such an
embarrassing defeat to the evil one.
For now, you who believe in my Son now hold all the
power over the evil one.

Oh, how wonderful My Son is.

I just had to ask the Light to tell me more about the
blood and what it meant.
The blood that flowed from My Son
is for the cleansing of all who want to be cleansed.
It will flow until My Son comes again.

I thought cleansed from what?

But the great I AM heard my thoughts and said to me
My precious Son's blood was shed to cleanse you of
<u>All</u> of your sins,
And I mean <u>ALL</u> of your sins past, present, and
future!
So you can look to a bright future with My Son!

THE FINE OLD TREE

Please remember the light said, I put on My Son <u>ALL</u>
of the world's sins, sickness, worries
and he nailed them to the cross (the Fine Old Tree)
with himself.
Look at how My Son took the sins of the world to the
cross with so much grace and courage.
What leadership! You would be wise to follow Him.

Oh, What Amazing Grace!

The Light then said I take what happened to My Son
on The Fine Old Tree very seriously!
He will not die for nothing!

What am I waiting for? I ran to that Fine Old Tree and
washed myself in the Red Flow.

What a Fine Old Tree we have!

THE FINE OLD TREE

Yet it pleased the Lord to bruise Him;
He has put Him to grief.
When You make His soul an offering for sin,
He shall see His seed, He shall prolong His days,
And the pleasure of the Lord shall prosper in His hand.
[11] He shall see the labor of His soul, and be satisfied.
By His knowledge, My righteous Servant shall justify
many,
For He shall bear their iniquities.
[12] Therefore I will divide Him a portion with the great,
And He shall divide the spoil with the strong,
Because He poured out His soul unto death,
And He was numbered with the transgressors,
And He bore the sin of many,
And made intercession for the transgressors.

Isaiah 53: 10-12

THE REASON FOR THE FINE OLD TREE

One day, the Holy Spirit whispered to my heart, revealing His sorrow for the Church. He grieved that many believers do not fully grasp the profound truth of the Cross of Jesus Christ. In His mercy, He called me to write a book that would illuminate its eternal significance. As I listened in reverence, He poured His words into me, guiding me to write and share these poems.

Then, the Spirit gave me another mission — to sell this book and dedicate all proceeds to restoring our church's Bell Tower. Our small congregation of 50 believers at Deering Center Community Church has prayed for a way to fund this need. Each purchase is an offering, ensuring the Bell Tower stands as a beacon of His presence.

Every year, our small church serves Jesus by providing thousands of meals and pieces of clothing to those in need.

If you feel led to support, we welcome you at Deering Center Community Church, 4 Brentwood Street, Portland, Maine 04013. May His grace uphold us all.

www.ingramcontent.com/pod-product-compliance
Lightning Source LLC
LaVergne TN
LVHW010027070426
835510LV00001B/12